To my parents (Phillip and Ella Mae Chapman) who passed away much too soon but who were my first inspiration to work hard and never give up on my dreams.

Songs of Love

My Little Bess Bean
A Poem For Sandy
A Song For Nancy
For Our Son
Sweet Lisa
The Golden Child
Dearest Sarah Bess
Dear Emily
The Prince and The Pauper
Dear Christopher
On Your Commencement
Welcome Aunt Lottie

Songs of Loss

What Can I Give
Farewell To My Aunt
Your Light Was Shining
Remembering Corine
Naomi's Songs
For Frankie
They Never Knew You
Despair
Left
Lost Dog
Lost Kitten
Sweet Ginny

MY LITTLE BESS BEAN

My Little Bess Bean
the little child within me
the light of my soul
still bright and shining
still hoping and trying
This body grown old
still looks to Bess Bean
the little child within me

You gave me strength to face
this speeding train through time and space
Together we passed through the best years
Together we enter the rest years
still looking for consolation even when mired in desolation
We walk together, souls linked forever
My little Bess Bean and me.

A POEM FOR SANDY

I never knew kids could cry all night
and still bring joy in the morning
And then came you.

I never knew kids could laugh and play
all day, every day
And then came you

I never knew kids could learn to do
so much so fast so well
And then came you

I never knew kids could be so good
at piano, violin, and tennis too
And then came you

I never knew kids could grow up,
win high honors at top schools
and become top docs
And then came you

I never knew the dream I had at 22
would come true
And then came you.

A SONG FOR NANCY

A dimpled, bubbly baby girl
catching sunbeams in her own little world
That was Nancy

A busy toddler, playing dolls
or so grown-up in heels and shawls
A quiet schoolgirl, a middle child
following and leading and dreaming and reading
and growing stronger all the while
That was Nancy

A golden teen, full of grace
at piano, tennis and anyplace
full of plans and determined to be
what all her dreams had let her see
That was Nancy

Now a young surgeon, loving and kind
who never left her sunbeams far behind
She brings them to us to warm our days
and keep us thankful and full of praise
for this precious gift
That is Nancy.

FOR OUR SON

So long ago when our world was new
with cries of joy we welcomed you.
At last a son had come to us
No wonder we danced and made a fuss
How could we know there was so much more?

Busy little curly headed boy
with so many toys and tape recorder noise,
searching, finding, unlocking doors
We did not know there was so much more.

A young boy playing with dogs and sisters too,
even then they brought their cares to you
Star student, sax player with the big Afro.
We did not know there was so much more.

Now a skilled surgeon and loving dad
who never lost the common touch.
For our family you always do so much,
you check on us all and answer any call.

Now we finally know and it is clear
how blessed we are to have you near
to lighten our loads and brighten our days.
And we thank whatever fates may be
that you are a part of this family.

And I know for sure that could never be
a better son than you to me.

SWEET LISA

You came to us, a sweet surprise,
with beautiful skin and hair and eyes,
a porcelain doll in the nursery
Adored from the first by the whole family.
Sweet Lisa, O how we welcomed you.

With Easter bunny birthdays and blue flower holidays,
you grew amazingly smart and talented too.
Young scholar, pianist, chess master, too,
Sweet Lisa, we were always so proud of you.

Now a young woman and mother of two,
your passion and love always shines through.
You still walk in beauty but lo and behold!
Your spirit runs deep and your heart is pure gold!

So busy helping and asking so little
and giving so much to the whole family.
But the greatest gift of all may be
when you sweet Lisa were given to me.
For in all the world there can never be
a more precious daughter than you are to me.

THE GOLDEN CHILD

Pushed too soon from your bed so warm
you slipped into our waiting arms,
with lungs so thin and limbs so weak
to yawn and sleep all through the dawn.

Then the sun came up and lit your face
with sparkling eyes and glowing smile
and you became a golden child.

Blood of African kings and Hebrew scholars
yet tinged with tears
from the Middle Passage and the Holocaust years.

Now young and safe within our fold,
one day you'll leave for dreams untold.
As the future becks and its call you heed,
generations before you bid you Godspeed.

So, go with courage and go with grace
with the wind at your back and the sun on your face.
With your sparkling eyes and glowing smile
you will always be our Golden Child.

DEAREST SARAH BESS

Dearest Sarah Bess,
How fitting that you should come to us
in this joyous holiday season
I bring to you three tokens of love,
a Christmas ball and embroidered bib,
and my baby silver spoon, all just for you...

Dearest Sarah Bess,
Blood of my blood, heart of my heart,
name of my name...
Take these gifts
from my arms to yours
as you came
from God's arms to mine....

DEAR EMILY

Dear Emily,
Welcome to this family
Now fair of face and full of grace
you had to fight for your time and space.
And we with furrowed brows did pray
for God's help to guide you on your way.
For every soul does have a place
if she stays the course and runs the race.
And when you came so quietly
we held our breaths so hopefully.
To us you looked so calm and wise
And we saw the sunshine in your eyes,
enough to warm cold winter days
and to light dark passageways.
You're sure to find your place to be
with your smiling eyes, Dear Emily,
Welcome to this family.

THE PRINCE AND THE PAUPER

A baby came into our world this year,
beautiful and healthy and loved so dear.
His family is wise and good of heart,
no cost need be spared to give him a good start.
His smile is merry, his eyes the same,
and we hold him close
Little Prince is his name.

A baby came into the world this year,
but none called him beautiful, nor wiped his tear
His family is poor, his start is drear.
His smile is sad, his eyes the same,
he is cast to the side
Little Pauper's his name.

But the little Prince will grow wise and soon discover,
that the wretched little Pauper is really his brother.
Like the great Frederick Douglass who roamed the South over,
who stood up for justice, the truth to be heard,
with mighty pen and thunderous word.

You, Douglass, too, may one day speak
to lift the downtrodden, and strengthen the weak.
So catch your sunbeams now, little Prince of fun,
the time will soon come for your work to be done.
Til then, we hold you and love you so dear,
and welcome you into our world this year.

DEAR CHRISTOPHER

Little one, son of my son
Our hearts were filled with wondrous joy
when we saw our beautiful baby boy.
But we cried hot tears when we knew
the pain and suffering you had to endure.
How could it be for one so new,
why couldn't we trade places with you?

There is so much we don't understand,
but it must be part of a bigger plan.
Maybe you had to cross the raging sea
to become the brave soul you were meant to be.

Each soul is passed through time and space,
on loan from God, a gift of grace.
It gives us courage each passing day
to meet the challenges along life's way.
And when we saw your smile and joie de vie,
we know how brave your soul must be.

And so, dear Chris, we take your hand
and walk with you as far as we can.
And when life calls you to take your place,
go with courage and go with grace.
Brave souls like your words from ages gone
will walk with you and lead you on.

ON YOUR COMMENCEMENT

On this happy day as you begin the journey to
adulthood, all those who love you wish for you all the
success you desire. Yet we both know for sure that
wishes won't make it so...What I do know for sure is
how lucky we are to be alive...What a tremendous
stroke of fate that out of the vastness of the universe,
a magical spark was ignited and we became part
of the miracle of life —
And from that moment on, to have escaped the
multitude of lurking dangers, and to arrive at
this time and space, that is indeed remarkable
and must be a gift from the Gods....

I do know for sure that this magnificent gift of
time is finite...it goes all too fast. It therefore seems
incumbent to respect and treasure every second of it.
And to decide early on to make the most of this
glorious journey ---
And these decisions must be yours and yours alone --- this is
your life —

Let no person or circumstance ever hijack your life.
Dream big, work hard, accept failure, and learn from it.
But never, ever give up on your dream, for dreams are the
driving force of life....

As you walk from us out into the wide panorama
of your life
which stretches further than our eyes can ever see,
promise me this one thing ---

That you will always love and believe in yourself
as much as we will always love and believe in you....

Bon Voyage, my Love --- Make a good life....

WELCOME AUNT LOTTIE

WELCOME, AUNT LOTTIE, on this Christmas 2009, to the family circle one more time. We have shared so much for so long, so many wonderful times, so many sad times. The saddest times were when the family circle was broken, but we closed ranks and supported each other every-time. You were there when our Dad passed away thirty years ago this Christmas. We were there when your son and nephew were so cruelly cut down some 25 years ago and also when my Mom and your Tom left us so terribly heartbroken.

But there have such wonderful times also. You stepped in to fill the void left by our own dear Mom, and we have loved you for it. You have celebrated with us through graduations, weddings, and new grand-babies.

Over the years, we have loved your delicious cooking....your sweet potato pies, your 'melt in the mouth' rolls that the kids fought over. We have appreciated your 'words of wisdom' so liberally given from child-rearing to bad hair to weight gain. If it needed saying, you said it! You have been the family historian, the only one left to give us the links to the past necessary to forge the bridge to the future.

You have been the brightest star on our Christmas tree for so many years. We are so thankful that you are here once again. We hope there will be many more festive occasions, But this may be the last time, we don't know. We do know that it will never be exactly the same. Time passes so fast. Next Christmas all of us will be changed, whether for better or worse, we don't know. This little time together is made all the sweeter because we know it is fleeting.

And so we join hands, and give thanks,
Aunt Lottie.
We love you, and we welcome you to the family
circle one more time.

SONGS OF LOSS

WHAT CAN I GIVE?

What can I give you? You, who gave me life, who fended off the boogeyman, and held my toddler's hand. You, who rose on cold winter mornings to light the bedroom fire so this schoolchild could wake up warm. You, who every day walked in the back door of The Man's factory to punch the 6 AM time clock, to put in eight hours of backbreaking blue-collar labor, every day, rain or shine, sick or well. You, who scratched out a living amidst the unrelenting prejudices of the Deep South. You, who had no more than a high school education, but who could work my college physics problems when I could not. You, who were determined that we should go further and taught me the glory of sacrifice, the beauty of the struggle, and the indomitability of the human spirit. What can I give you?

They told us two years ago that it was myeloma and that the usual prognosis for this kind was just two years. But we said we would give it a good fight. And we did. My knees shaking, I held your hand at your first chemotherapy treatment. You said the medicine burned as it into your veins, and you were so sick afterwards.

But we had two good years, the birthdays, the holidays, the just plain days when we sat on the porch and talked. We talked about the old days when I was little and you were young. And oh, what a memory you had... You could remember 40 years back, the exact time of year, the exact day, oh, the wonder of such a gift.

But we could all see you were getting weaker. The hospital stays were longer, and more frequent, and we knew. We avoided direct eye contact less the other see what we both knew.

Now as I keep the visual by your hospital bed and you fitfully sleep, I tiptoe up, check the Foley catheter and the cut-down, as your veins have long since collapsed. I pat your shoulder, and try not to think of what it would be like without you. Oh, how can I bear never again to see your face, to hear your voice? My house will be cold and small and I shall search for you in this all its pitiful corners. How can I bear to find you not?

And I wonder... What can I give you? And you wake to speak, and my tears flow freely. We tell you that we love you, that we won't leave you. And you nod your and hoarsely whisper "I know you did all you could for me and I did all I could for you."

And now I know what I can give. I can do for myself what you could not do for me 20 years ago. I can once again undertake plans for medical education, impossible then because we had no money. I can endure the long years of hard work, and worse still the anxiety of possible failure. And it will still be far less than you endured.

And then I can give to those poor old sick ones like you, who come, stooped and gnarled, to these rough places, so many without even a hand to hold. If I can ease their pain, if I can soothe their passing, I shall be content. For in them, I may once again see your face in the oneness of the universe.

My father passed this life on December 17, 1979. I entered medical school in 1980.

FAREWELL TO MY AUNT

You always knew how much we loved you.
But did you know how much we thank you?
You did so much for so many for so long.
Yet we never told you how much we thank you.
And so in this farewell we thank you now.
For when you were just 10 years old how
you took your baby brother
to tend him, to love him, to stand by him until he passed.
That baby was our dad we thank you now.
For how you taught four little girls so much, not just
to bake a better cake, or to sew a finer seam,
but how to live a better life.
Those four little girls were us and for that we
thank you now.
For when your beloved brother and his wife fell ill,
how you came to help out and stayed on until the end.
Those were our parents and for that we thank you now.
And when we were all grownup and could look back,
we saw how special you really were; how even though
small and soft-spoken,

you were blessed with a mind as clear as the
finest diamond and with a spirit as tough as the
strongest steel.
We knew then that you were one for the ages.
You, who worked so hard in life, who faced so
much personal loss,
yet always willing to pick up the yoke to lighten
another's load.
You taught us that we, too, can face adversity,
and still reach out to brighten dark corners.

Farewell, Dear Aunt,
You always knew how much we loved you
and now you know how much we thank you.

YOUR LIGHT WAS SHINING

Your light came up at the turn of the century,
number nine of twelve, just one of many
And even then, your light was shining

From the time you were the elegant New York lady
who sent Christmas treasures and Easter pleasures
to the times when we talked and laughed
at all the tales you told so well
Your light was shining

To the many times you gave comfort
when all the others slipped away
and we wept hot tears in dark places
Your light was shining

And your light was so loved and so blessed
to shine brighter and longer than all the rest
And since no light is ever lost,
but blends in wondrous majesty
Now we may look up and see
Your light shines in eternity

REMEMBERING CORINE

I will remember Corine as she was when I first met her, both of us young wives married to first cousins. The cousins were like brothers and we became like sisters. She was so devoted to her family, so proud of her husband and son, but especially proud of her grandkids. They both knew how much she loved them, and how special she was....

I, too, will remember how special Corine was to us. She was always so generous, not just to us, but to the many house guests we brought to the cabin, always welcoming them with home-baked treats or flower cuttings from her garden. That's how special Corine was.....

I will remember the many happy times we shared --- graduations, weddings and vacations. She especially loved those vacations.

We loved Corine and she knew it.....

But we also knew that she gave us much more than we could ever give her. The truth was, it was our pleasure to be with her, for she was one of these rare persons whose true value is not measured in social status or material things. Corine cared nothing for them.
The measure of the value of such a person is in how many lives are touched, and made better by it.
Corine touched lives and made them better.
She saw heavy loads and made them lighter.
She saw dark corners and made them brighter.....

Corine toiled long and hard in the vineyard.
Her work on this earth is done now. But all of us here can see her life as a shining example of a life well-lived, a race well run, a job well done....

Farewell, dear Corine, my sister, my friend. I will miss you. But I will always remember you as a sweet sweet spirit who tried to help somebody along life's way

NAOMI'S SONGS

We were friends as college freshmen, Naomi and I, she in the arts, I in the sciences. I first heard her singing in the college choir "There is a Balm in Gilead". Nobody could sing that song like Naomi. That was Naomi's song. She also raised our sorority hymn to celestial heights, and that too was Naomi's song.

Through the years we celebrated the joys of marriage and motherhood, our pride and love for our families; we grieved over the loss of our parents, our siblings, our friends. When she became ill, she fought the good fight and we stood together. Through all her life she walked in beauty and courage.

I never heard her sing again, but Naomi's songs are not gone from us; they can never be lost. For a life is a miracle of the universe, ever turning, moving through time and space throughout eternity. Nothing is ever lost from the universe, no drop of rain nor grain of sand...

We will still hear Naomi's songs in all the wonders of life, in the soft touch of the first spring day, in the trill of a nesting songbird, in the sigh of a sleeping baby. For these are all songs of beauty, songs of life.

These are all Naomi's songs.

FOR FRANKIE

It floated so light onto my palm,
its little wings yellow, so light, so bright.
It lingered but a moment there, resting,
its little heart beating so softly,
its little wings opening, closing...

This miracle of life that I may hold but a moment,
Please stay, please stay
I cup my palm over its ephemeral softness.....

It flutters s its little wings
so light, so bright
and floats away to Golden Meadows
that mortal eyes shall never see
leaving behind on my beseeching palm
a bit of yellow dust
so light so bright

THEY NEVER KNEW YOU

They never knew you,
flushed away in a fetal sac,
just another life that could not be.

But I knew you.
And gloried in the secret within me
and moaned the fluttering goodbye kicks.
Yes, I knew you and did try to give you life...

But, oh, the treasures you gave to me,
not just the blooming of my body
but the blooming of my soul.

A promise of new tomorrows,
a promise, which though now, can never be,
glows in the memory.
And like you, will forever be
part of me.

DESPAIR

His hands lie folded on a bier
No more to reach out across the way
Nor bruise and bleed from life's cruel play
His eyes no more to gaze at Spring's first bloom
Nor spill hot tears for hopes grown dim
His feet no more to chase the Summer dream
Nor falter in the heavy clay
His heart no more to thrill at the first robin's call
Nor despair at love's shortfall
Tired of searching for his place to be
He slipped the surly bonds of earth
And rests eternally.

LEFT

With a hurt so deep
that even in sleep
hot tears fall drop by drop
upon my heart
Til awful truth
is truth redeemed
through the awesome
Grace of God

LOST DOG

No more than a general tail wag to fingers softly snapped
the answering lope to manly whistle
No more the fateful mascot following
a boy and girl in chill morning air,
the sad eyes watchful as the school bus
leaves a spot where they stood,
and roars on.
No more to lie and wait in thin winter sun
til that same roar announces the joyful return
No more the playful romp on dead grasses —
the happy growl when tugging at a child's sleeve
the boisterous bark when racing boys bikes
The lively playmate is
No more

LOST KITTEN

Will someone hear her

softly crying in the frozen winter night?

will someone who look at her

and think her beautiful as I did?

Will someone feed her and warm her and comfort her

will someone love her as I did?

SWEET GINNY

She came to me unbidden,
scrawny, full of fleas, a shelter kitten.
But underneath she was glossy black and beautiful
and full of life.
Kitty Ginny jumped so high to porch, piano and
swinging chairs.
She played with the grandkids and they napped on the floor
Grown Ginny rambled outside with our dog
in the warmth of summer
and snoozed in a soft chair in the cold of winter.
Then Ginny was twenty and we celebrated her.
She slept on the floor bathed in sunbeams
or behind the sofa near the cool air vent.
She still loved our nightly ritual of brushing and petting.
She smoothed the rough edges of my day as much as I
soothed her.
In the last days I rubbed her head and kept her comfortable.
We all loved her but she was my baby
Goodbye, sweet Ginny
I will miss you mightily.

Acknowledgements:

Thanks to my husband of over sixty years, Herbert, for his support in so many of my projects along our journey. He and my son, Herb, encouraged me to complete this manuscript and also typed, formatted, and proof read for me. Thanks to Javon, my brother-in-law, who helped to navigate and smooth the road for this first time publisher.

Special acknowledgments to all my family who so touched my life and filled my heart with song. My four adult children (Sandy, Nancy, Herbie, and Lisa) and five grandchildren (Micheal, Sarah, Emily, Douglass, and Christopher) have all inspired songs of celebration and hope. Old aunts who lived long and rich lives taught me so much; they certainly deserve songs of love and appreciation. But so many who enriched my life are gone now; they too are remembered here in songs of mournful loss.

In the end love and loss will round out all our days.
For these are indeed all songs of life.

Made in the USA
Columbia, SC
13 April 2022

58940277R00031